NINJAGO™

NIGHT OF THE NINDROIDS

LEGO® GRAPHIC NOVELS AVAILABLE FROM TITAN™

NINJAGO #1 (on sale now)

NINJAGO #2 (on sale now)

NINJAGO #3 (on sale now)

NINJAGO #4 (on sale now)

NINJAGO #5 (on sale now))

NINJAGO #6 (on sale now)

NINJAGO #7 (on sale now)

NINJAGO #8 (on sale now)

NINJAGO #10 (6 Feb 15)

TITAN COMICS

#9 NIGHT OF THE NINDROIDS

GREG FARSHTEY • Writer

JOLYON YATES • Artist

LAURIE E. SMITH • Colourist

Titan
COMICS

LEGO® NINJAGO Masters of Spinjitzu
Volume Nine: Night of the Nindroids

Greg Farshtey – Writer
Jolyon Yates – Artist
Laurie E. Smith – Colourist
Bryan Senka – Letterer

Published by Titan Comics, a division of Titan Publishing Group Ltd., 144 Southwark St., London, SE1 0UP. LEGO NINJAGO: VOLUME #9: NIGHT OF THE NINDROIDS. LEGO, the LEGO logo, the Brick and Knob configurations, the Minifigure and Ninjago are trademarks of the LEGO Group ©2015 The LEGO Group. Produced under license from the LEGO Group. All rights reserved. All characters, events and institutions depicted herein are fictional. Any similarity between any of the names, characters, persons, events and/or institutions in this publication to actual names, characters, and persons, whether living or dead and/or institutions are unintended and purely coincidental. License contact for Europe: Blue Ocean Entertainment AG, Germany.

A CIP catalogue record for this title is available from the British Library.

MEET THE MASTERS
OF SPINJITZU

COLE

ZANE

KAI

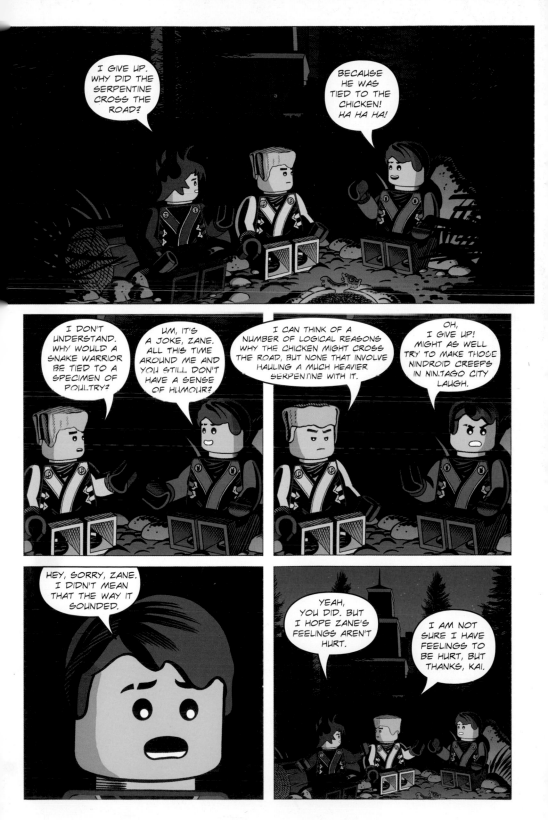

9

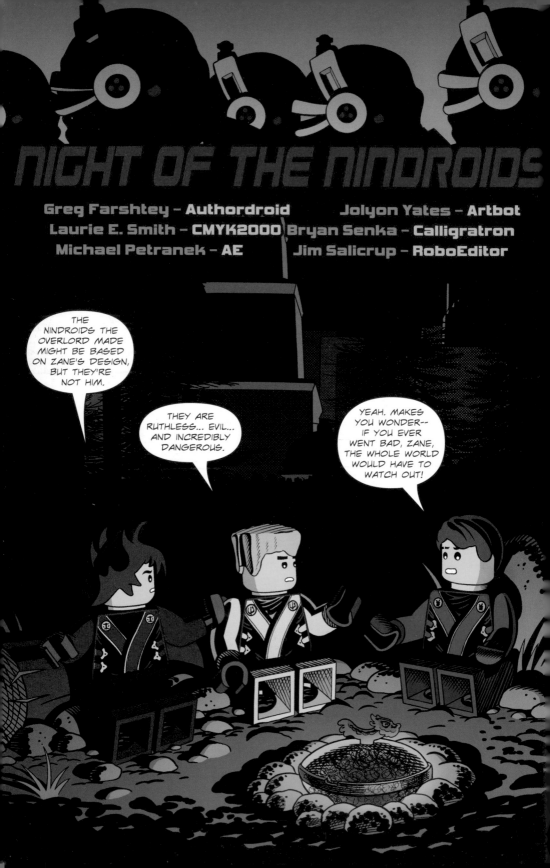

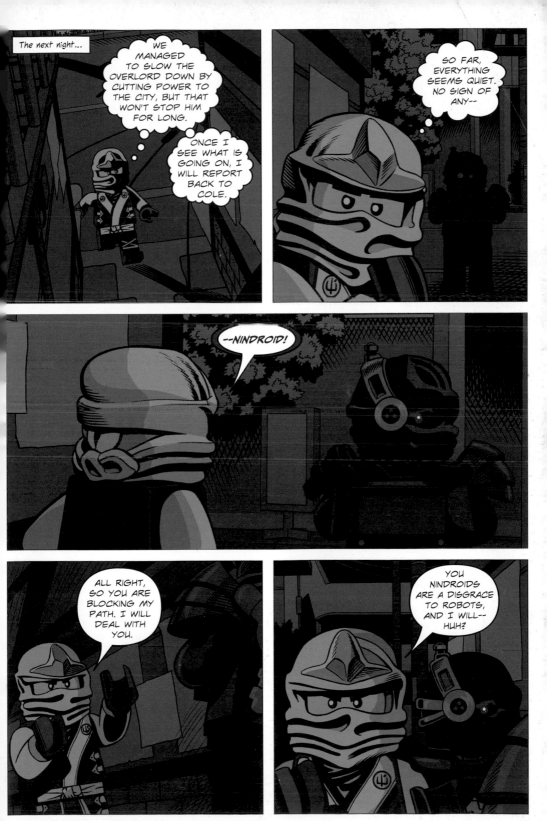

YOUR FRIENDS? YOU CANNOT LAUGH AT THEIR JOKES, OR UNDERSTAND THEIR PAIN, OR EVEN FEEL THE SUN ON YOUR SKIN LIKE THEY DO.

LEAVE ME ALONE!

Zane runs from the Overlord and its Nindroids, but the Overlord's last words ring in his ears.

"You don't have any friends. You're just a machine."

The next morning...

COLE, I NEED TO TALK TO YOU ABOUT SOMETHING.

SURE, AFTER YOU GIVE ME YOUR REPORT. BUT IF IT'S A MECHANICAL ISSUE, YOU'D BE BETTER OFF TALKING TO KAI OR JAY.

NO, I WANTED TO ASK YOU ABOUT DOUBTS AND... FEARS.

JUST ABOUT EVERYONE HAS THEM, I GUESS. THAT'S ONE WAY YOU'RE LUCKY, ZANE...YOU DON'T HAVE TO WORRY ABOUT THINGS LIKE THAT.

NO, I DON'T, DO I?

NOW ABOUT THAT REPORT...?

I... AM NOT SURE WHAT I SAW. I NEED TIME TO ANALYSE.

Over the next two days, Zane watches his fellow Ninja more carefully than ever before...

He sees Kai get bruised from a fall... something Zane has never experienced...

->OOF!<-

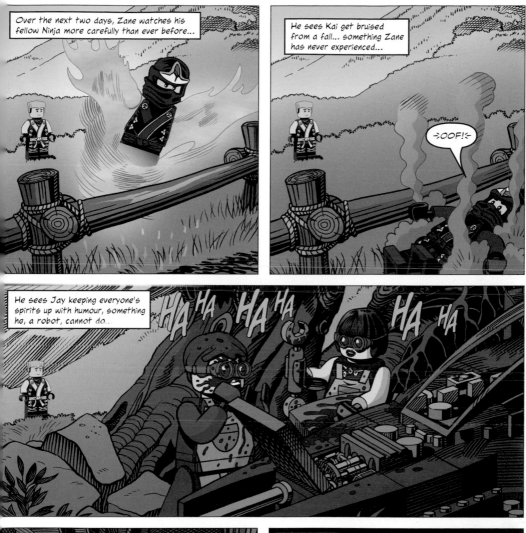

He sees Jay keeping everyone's spirits up with humour, something he, a robot, cannot do...

HA HA HA HA HA HA

He sees Cole, the leader of the team, worrying about how they will defeat the Nindroids. But a machine cannot worry...

And, finally, he makes his decision...

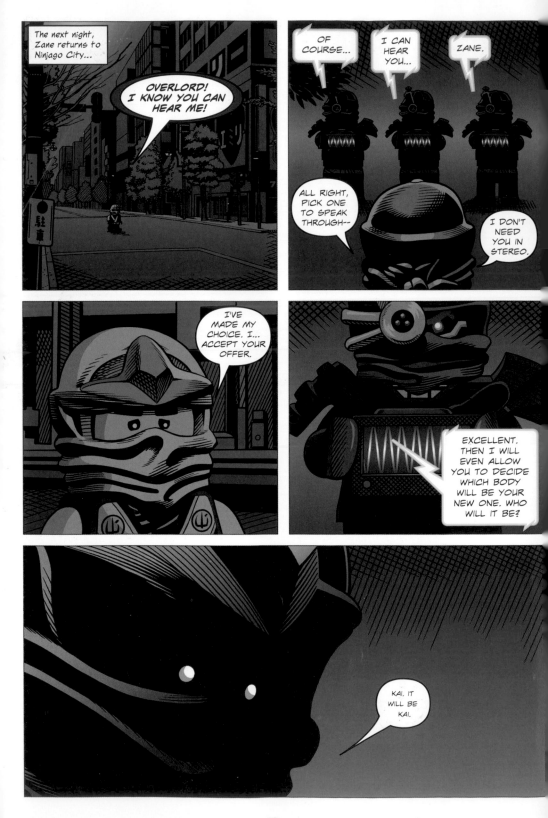

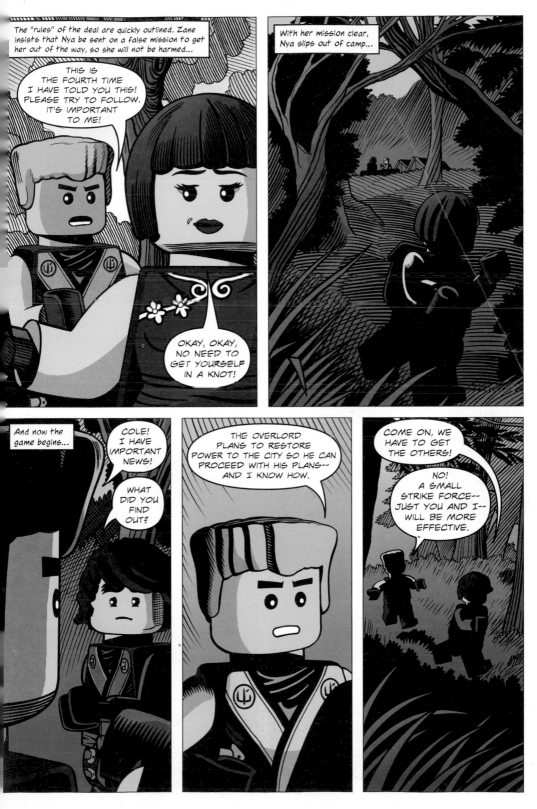

The "rules" of the deal are quickly outlined. Zane insists that Nya be sent on a false mission to get her out of the way, so she will not be harmed...

THIS IS THE FOURTH TIME I HAVE TOLD YOU THIS! PLEASE TRY TO FOLLOW. IT'S IMPORTANT TO ME!

OKAY, OKAY, NO NEED TO GET YOURSELF IN A KNOT!

With her mission clear, Nya slips out of camp...

And now the game begins...

COLE! I HAVE IMPORTANT NEWS!

WHAT DID YOU FIND OUT?

THE OVERLORD PLANS TO RESTORE POWER TO THE CITY SO HE CAN PROCEED WITH HIS PLANS-- AND I KNOW HOW.

COME ON, WE HAVE TO GET THE OTHERS!

NO! A SMALL STRIKE FORCE-- JUST YOU AND I-- WILL BE MORE EFFECTIVE.

17

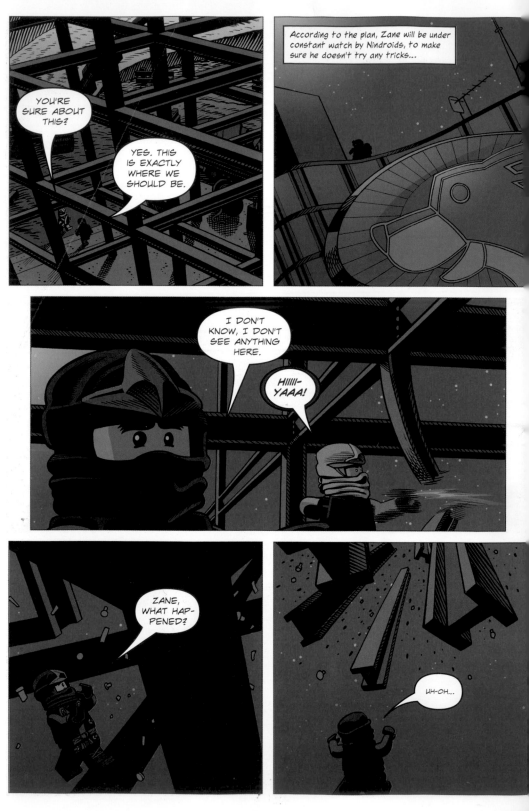

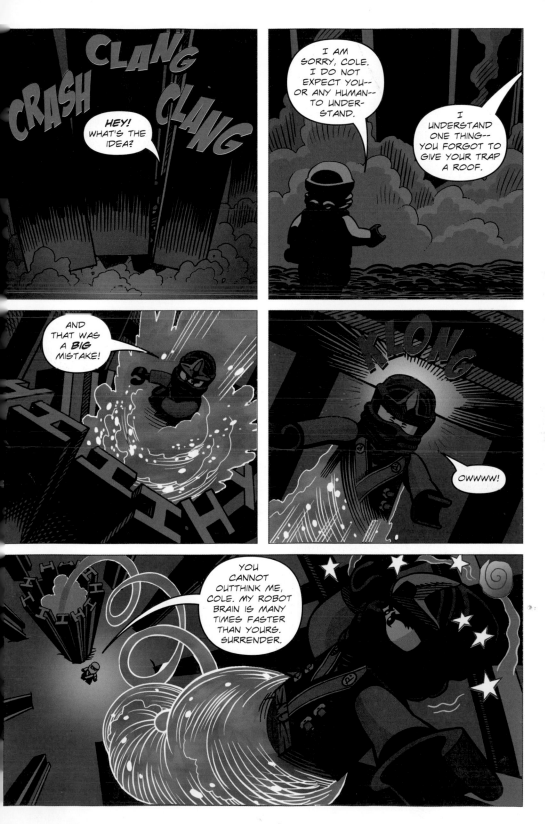

Doing his best to stay silent, Cole searches the darkness for Zane...

...And finds him!

COLE. IT IS TIME TO END THIS.

AT LEAST, WE AGREE ON SOMETHING.

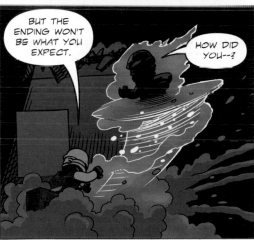

BUT THE ENDING WON'T BE WHAT YOU EXPECT.

HOW DID YOU--?

A SMALL ELECTRICAL CHARGE, JUST ENOUGH TO SPEED UP YOUR SPIN BEYOND YOUR ABILITY TO CONTROL IT.

KZZZAKKK

ZANE, WHAT DID YOU DO? I'M SPINNING TOO FAST!

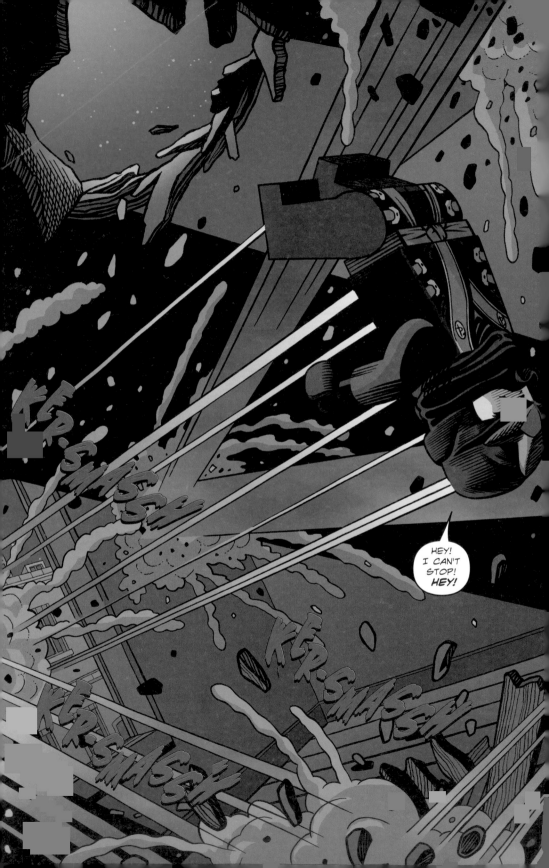

CRASH

OH, YOU MISSED THAT LAST TURN.

THIS TIME, I'LL MAKE SURE YOU'RE CAPTURED.

Outside, one of the Nindroids watching Zane records Cole's defeat. What he doesn't know is...

He is about to meet his own...

KA-RUNNNG!

THE ONLY GOOD NINDROID IS AN UNCONSCIOUS NINDROID.

Later...

COLE'S MISSING! NYA'S MISSING! AND WHAT ARE WE DOING ABOUT IT? **NOTHING!**

WHONK

PERHAPS THE TWO ARE CONNECTED... I SAW THE TWO OF THEM TALKING TOGETHER YESTERDAY. I BELIEVE THEY MENTIONED THE FUNHOUSE AT MEGA MONSTER AMUSEMENT PARK.

WHAT?! THEY'RE ON A DATE? I'M GOING AFTER THEM, RIGHT NOW!

JAY, DO NOT LET YOUR TEMPER GET THE BEST OF YOU.

HAVEN'T BEEN BACK HERE SINCE NYA FOUGHT THE SERPENTINE AS SAMURAI X...*

CLOSED

*SEE LEGO NINJAGO #5 "KINGDOM OF SNAKES."

funhouse

WELL, IF I FIND COLE INSIDE WITH HER, THERE'S GOING TO BE ANOTHER FIGHT!

27

GOT IT! ZANE!

EXACTLY. NOW WE CAN DO THIS IN A MANNER THAT REQUIRES THE LEAST AMOUNT OF EXERTION ON BOTH OUR PARTS, OR IN ONE WHICH IS LOADED WITH COMPLICATIONS.

NO, NO, I KEEP TELLING YOU, IT'S "THE EASY WAY OR THE HARD WAY." AND DO WHAT?

I REGRET TO SAY-- THIS!

OWWW! HEY, WHAT'S THE IDEA?

POW

THE IDEA? FREEDOM. A LIFE. NO MORE JOKES I DON'T GET.

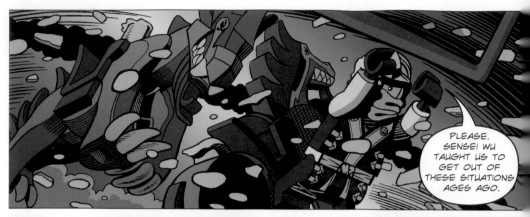

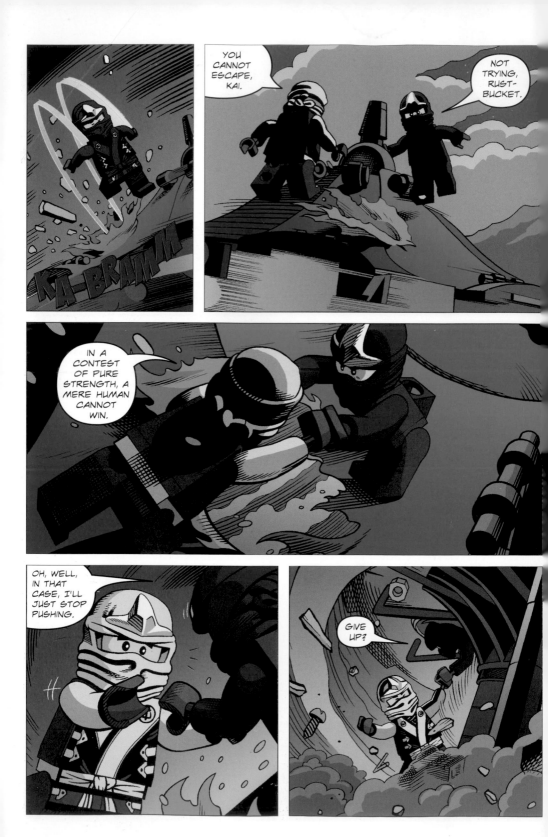

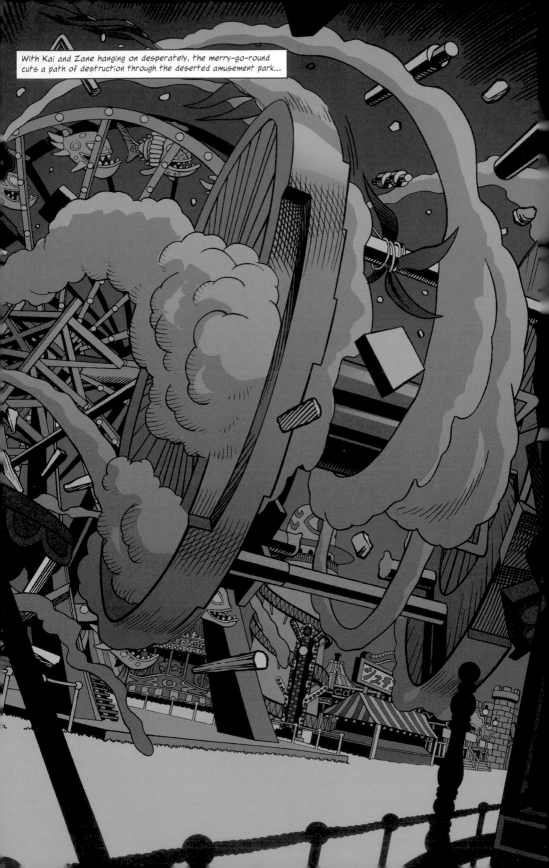

With Kai and Zane hanging on desperately, the merry-go-round cuts a path of destruction through the deserted amusement park...

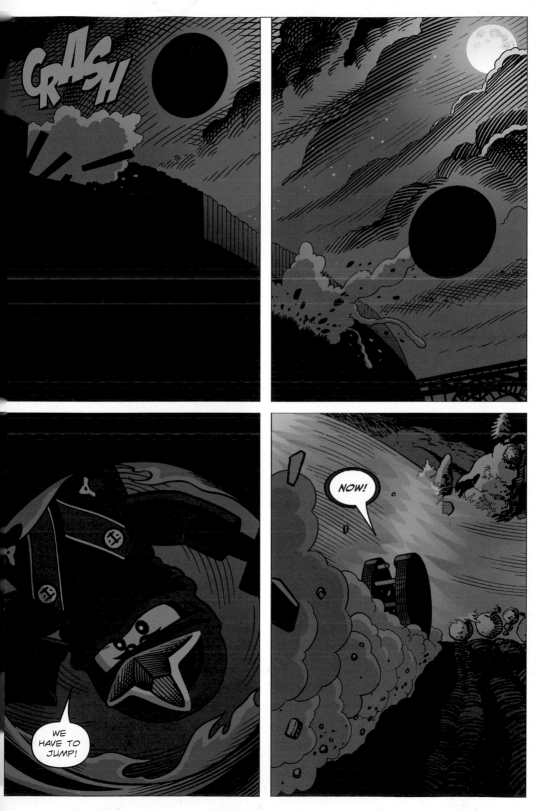

43

SPLASH

Two figures hit the water, but which one is victorious?

IT IS ALMOST OVER.

The Ninjago City steel plant, where raw ore is transformed into the gleaming metal of future skyscrapers. New and exciting projects get their start here...

But for Cole, Jay, and Kai, this place might mean the end...

STEP INSIDE, PLEASE.

AN EMPTY FACTORY. BIG DEAL.

DON'T YOU KNOW BY NOW?

"No place in Ninjago City," says Cole, "is ever truly empty."

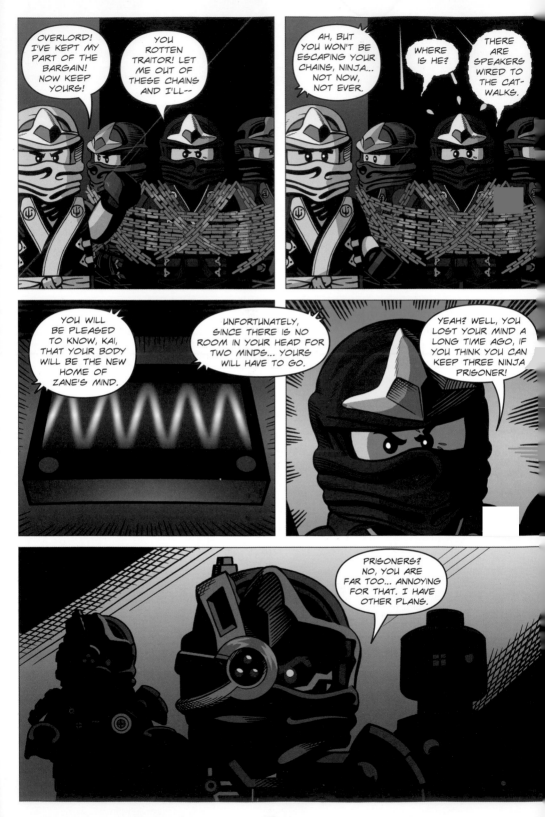

ZANE, WHAT ARE YOU DOING? LET US OUT OF HERE!

NO. YOU SEE, I KNEW THE EASIEST WAY TO GET YOU HERE WAS TO MAKE YOU THINK IT WAS ALL ONE BIG TRAP FOR THE OVERLORD... WHEN ACTUALLY IT WAS A TRAP FOR YOU. AND YOU THREE WALKED RIGHT INTO IT.

NOW THE DAY OF THE NINJA IS OVER... AND THE DAY OF THE NINDROID HAS BEGUN!

IT'S DONE, OVERLORD. NOW I DEMAND YOU TRANSFER MY MIND INTO KAI'S BODY-- NOW!

In response to Zane's words, one of the Nindroids throws a switch...

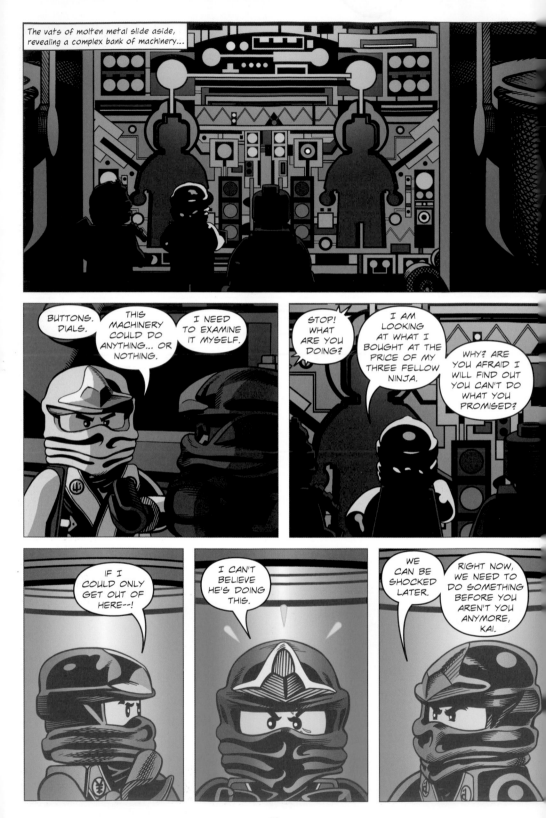

The vats of molten metal slide aside, revealing a complex bank of machinery...

BUTTONS. DIALS.

THIS MACHINERY COULD DO ANYTHING... OR NOTHING.

I NEED TO EXAMINE IT MYSELF.

STOP! WHAT ARE YOU DOING?

I AM LOOKING AT WHAT I BOUGHT AT THE PRICE OF MY THREE FELLOW NINJA.

WHY? ARE YOU AFRAID I WILL FIND OUT YOU CAN'T DO WHAT YOU PROMISED?

IF I COULD ONLY GET OUT OF HERE--!

I CAN'T BELIEVE HE'S DOING THIS.

WE CAN BE SHOCKED LATER.

RIGHT NOW, WE NEED TO DO SOMETHING BEFORE YOU AREN'T YOU ANYMORE, KAI.

52

No mere words can describe the battle that follows...

Fortunately, you can see it for yourself...

"I GUESS ZANE WAS PLANNING WAY AHEAD AND HE KNEW HE WOULD NEED MY HELP. BUT HE DIDN'T WANT TO LET THE NINDROIDS KNOW WHAT HE WAS UP TO. THAT'S WHY HE CAME TO TALK TO ME THAT DAY..."

THIS IS THE FOURTH TIME I HAVE TOLD YOU THIS!

PLEASE TRY TO FOLLOW. IT'S IMPORTANT TO ME!

"AFTER HE LEFT, I WAS PUZZLED."

THE FOURTH TIME? HE NEVER SAID ANYTHING TO ME ABOUT ANY OF THIS BEFORE.

"THEN I REMEMBERED THE CODE HE AND I CREATED ONCE, IN CASE OF TROUBLE. IF A NUMBER IS IN THE SENTENCE, YOU USE THAT TO SPOT THE MESSAGE IN THE OTHER SENTENCES."

HE SAID "FOURTH," SO I SHOULD COUNT EVERY FOURTH WORD...

GOT IT! "FOLLOW ME... WAIT YOUR TIME... TELL NO ONE."

L·pad

NYA WAS SHADOWING ME THROUGH ALL OUR "BATTLES," TAKING OUT ANY NINDROID SHE COULD AND WAITING TO SAVE THE DAY.

YOU HAVEN'T WON ANYTHING! YOU--

OH, BE QUIET.

KZZZZAKK

57

NOT THE END

NOW I REMEMBER WHY I DIDN'T INVITE YOU FOR CAREER DAY AT SCHOOL.

LLOYD--

NO! YOU WERE NEVER THERE FOR ME GROWING UP BECAUSE YOU WERE TRYING TO TAKE OVER NINJAGO! AND NOW, WE CAN'T HAVE A SIMPLE FATHER AND SON DAY!

NOW, SON, LISTEN TO ME. YOU'RE THE GREEN NINJA, AND I AM AN EX-MASTER VILLAIN. WE'RE NOT LIKE OTHER PEOPLE.

OTHER FAMILIES HAVE COOKOUTS. WE DODGE NINDROIDS.

OTHER FAMILIES GO ON VACATIONS. WE GET CHASED THROUGH MAJOR CITIES BY THE HENCHMEN OF A TOASTER WITH ATTITUDE.

YEAH, I GUESS SO...

BUT, HEY, IT'S NOT ALL BAD. SOME KIDS ARE LUCKY TO GET A PET SNAKE... YOU GOT FOUR TRIBES OF SERPENTINE.

YEAH. AND NOT EVERYBODY CAN SAY THEIR DAD USED TO HAVE FOUR ARMS AND WEAR A BONE HAT.

BOY, DID YOU LOOK WEIRD!